BASEBALL LEGENDS

Hank Aaron
Grover Cleveland Alexander
Ernie Banks
Johnny Bench
Yogi Berra
Roy Campanella
Roberto Clemente
Ty Cobb
Dizzy Dean
Joe DiMaggio
Bob Feller
Jimmie Foxx
Lou Gehrig
Bob Gibson
Rogers Hornsby
Walter Johnson
Sandy Koufax
Mickey Mantle
Christy Mathewson
Willie Mays
Stan Musial
Satchel Paige
Brooks Robinson
Frank Robinson
Jackie Robinson
Babe Ruth
Duke Snider
Warren Spahn
Willie Stargell
Honus Wagner
Ted Williams
Carl Yastrzemski
Cy Young

CHELSEA HOUSE PUBLISHERS

BASEBALL LEGENDS

ROBERTO CLEMENTE

Peter C. Bjarkman

Introduction by
Jim Murray

Senior Consultant
Earl Weaver

CHELSEA HOUSE PUBLISHERS

New York • Philadelphia

Published by arrangement with
Chelsea House Publishers.
Newfield Publications is a federally
registered trademark of Newfield
Publications, Inc.

Produced by James Charlton Associates
New York, New York.

Designed by Hudson Studio
Ossining, New York.

Typesetting by LinoGraphics
New York, New York.

Picture research by Carolann Hawkins
Cover illustration by Dan O'Leary

Library of Congress Cataloging-in-Publication Data

Bjarkman, Peter C.
    Roberto Clemente Peter C. Bjarkman; introd. by Jim Murray.
  p. cm.—(Baseball legends)
  Includes bibliographical references and index.
    Summary: A biography of the baseball superstar from Puerto
Rico who, before his untimely death in a 1972 airplane crash, was
noted for his achievements on and off the baseball field.
  ISBN 0-7910-1171-2.—ISBN 0-7910-1205-0 (pbk.)
  1. Clemente, Roberto, 1934-1972—Juvenile literature. 2. Baseball
players—Puerto Rico—Biography—Juvenile literature. 3. Pittsburgh
Pirates (Baseball team) —Juvenile literature. [1. Clemente, Roberto,
1934-1972. 2. Baseball players. 3. Blacks—Puerto Rico— Biography.]
  I. Title.   II. Series.
  GV865.C45B53 1991
  92—dc20   90-47127
  796.357'092   CIP
  [B]   AC

CONTENTS

WHAT MAKES A STAR

Jim Murray

No one has ever been able to explain to me the mysterious alchemy that makes one man a .350 hitter and another player, more or less identical in physical makeup, hard put to hit .200. You look at an Al Kaline, who played with the Detroit Tigers from 1953 to 1974. He was pale, stringy, almost poetic-looking. He always seemed to be struggling against a bad case of mononucleosis. But with a bat in his hands, he was King Kong. During his career, he hit 399 home runs, rapped out 3,007 hits, and compiled a .297 batting average.

Form isn't the reason. The first time anybody saw Roberto Clemente step into the batter's box for the Pittsburgh Pirates, the best guess was that Clemente would be back in Double A ball in a week. He had one foot in the bucket and held his bat at an awkward angle—he looked as though he couldn't hit an outside pitch. A lot of other ballplayers may have had a better-looking stance. Yet they never led the National League in hitting in four different years, the way Clemente did.

Not every ballplayer is born with the ability to hit a curveball. Nor is exceptional hand-eye coordination the key to heavy hitting. Big-league locker rooms are filled with players who have all the attributes, save one: discipline. Every baseball man can tell you a story about a pitcher who throws a ball faster than anyone has ever seen but who has no control on or *off* the field.

The Hall of Fame is full of people who transformed themselves into great ballplayers by working at the sport, by studying the game, and making sacrifices. They're overachievers—and winners. If you want to find them, just watch the World Series. Or simply read about New York Yankee great Lou Gehrig; Ted Williams, "the Splendid Splinter" of the Boston Red Sox; or the Dodgers' strikeout king Sandy Koufax.

A pitcher *should* be able to win a lot of ballgames with a 98-miles-per-hour fastball. But what about the pitcher who wins 20 games a year with a fastball so slow that you can catch it with your teeth? Bob Feller of the Cleveland Indians got into the Hall of Fame with a blazing fastball that glowed in the dark. National League star Grover Cleveland Alexander got there with a pitch that took considerably longer to reach the plate; but when it did arrive, the pitch was exactly where Alexander wanted it to be—and the last place the batter expected it to be.

There are probably more players with exceptional ability who didn't make it to the major leagues than there are who did. A number of great hitters, bored with fielding practice, had to be dropped from their team because their home-run production didn't make up for their lapses in the field. And then there are players like Brooks Robinson of the Baltimore Orioles, who made himself into a human vacuum cleaner at third base because he knew that working hard to become an expert fielder would win him a job in the big leagues.

A star is not something that flashes through the sky. That's a comet. Or a meteor. A star is something you can steer ships by. It stays in place and gives off a steady glow; it is fixed, permanent. A star works at being a star.

And that's how you tell a star in baseball. He shows up night after night and takes pride in how brightly he shines. He's Willie Mays running so hard his hat keeps falling off; Ty Cobb sliding to stretch a single into a double; Lou Gehrig, after being fooled in his first two at-bats, belting the next pitch off the light tower because he's taken the time to study the pitcher. Stars never take themselves for granted. That's why they're stars.

THE SUPERSTAR

Opening Day is always a time for renewed hope. For every big-league baseball team and its fans, the start of a new season means another chance to take part in an exciting pennant race. When the 1955 baseball campaign began in Pittsburgh, Pennsylvania, however, the local fans had little reason to expect any great changes in what had by then become a legacy of losing seasons and uninspired play.

For the past three years—and four out of the past five—the Pirates had finished in last place in the National League. The team had not come in higher than fourth place since 1944, when it had finished second. The last Pittsburgh team to win a pennant played in 1927, the year that Babe Ruth hit 60 home runs as part of the New York Yankees' "Murderers' Row."

The Pirates' one bright spot on Opening Day of the 1955 season was the debut of 20-year-old Puerto Rican sensation Roberto Clemente. When he first stepped into the batter's box at

Clemente climbs the fence in San Francisco's Candlestick Park attempting to catch a drive off the bat of Hobie Landrith.

Pittsburgh's Forbes Field on Sunday, April 17, to face the Brooklyn Dodgers' lefthander Johnny Podres, he rapped out a sharp infield grounder that was too hot to be handled cleanly by shortstop Pee Wee Reese. Moments later, Clemente scored on Frank Thomas's long triple. By the time the day was over, Clemente had registered three base hits, including a double, in his National League debut.

To prove that his first afternoon's work was no mere fluke, Clemente smacked an inside-the-park homer the very next day against New York Giants hurler Don Liddle at the Polo Grounds. The promising rookie was hitting .360, seventh best in the league, by week's end, and had made several fine fielding plays.

Like many young ballplayers, Clemente seemed eager to swing at almost any pitch. His strike zone, one sportswriter noted, seemed to extend from the first-base dugout to the third-base dugout. He also bobbed his head so violently when he swung that he took his eye off the ball.

"The first time I ever saw him," Hall of Fame pitcher Robin Roberts said, "he came up to hit and I turned to someone and said, 'Who is this?' That was back when the Pirates were first bringing up a lot of different young guys. They even tried Tony Bartirome, their trainer, at first base one year. And it looked like Roberto was another one of these guys. He looked less like a ballplayer than anyone I've ever seen."

But Clemente's looks were deceiving. Unlike most free-swingers, he consistently made good contact and hit for a high average. Year in and year out, he was a threat to win the National League batting title. All told, he won it four times, finishing with a lifetime batting average of .317. In

Clemente routinely made spectacular catches to take away hits. During his career, he won 12 Gold Gloves, the award instituted in 1957 to honor the top fielders.

1972, he became only the eleventh player in baseball history to rap out 3,000 career base hits.

The excitement that Clemente generated was not simply a matter of possessing an explosive bat. He was also a daring baserunner. The sight of Clemente tearing around the base paths, legging out an extra-base hit, was a thrilling experience. Only a few players, among them Jackie Robinson, the first black to play major league baseball, ever ran the bases as aggressively as Clemente did.

On top of his hitting and baserunning, Clemente was perhaps the finest defensive right fielder the sport has ever seen. On his way to winning 12 Gold Glove Awards, he played the outfield with incomparable grace and an amazing amount of daring. Indeed, few players have ever created so much excitement when fielding balls hit to the outfield.

Clemente's cannon-like throwing arm was what first attracted legions of big-league scouts to Puerto Rico to watch him play when he was 18. His arm was as accurate as it was powerful, and he went on to lead all National League outfielders in assists five times. He specialized in cutting down runners who attempted to advance from first to third on a base hit. His favorite play, though, was to rifle a throw to the first baseman after a batter had singled to right and then made too wide a turn at first base. More often than the other team would like, Clemente would nail the embarrassed runner.

By the time Clemente's 18-year career came to an end in 1972, he had played in a dozen straight All-Star Games, starred in two World Series triumphs, and won the National League's 1966 Most Valuable Player Award. He had also become the Pittsburgh Pirates' all-time leader in games played, at-bats, hits, singles, total bases, and runs batted in. Leading in all those categories was quite an accomplishment, because a number of Hall of Famers had already played for the Pittsburgh franchise, including Max Carey, Ralph Kiner, Honus Wagner, Paul and Lloyd Waner, and Pie Traynor.

And yet playing major league baseball was not always an easy task for Clemente. When the Puerto Rican native first joined the big leagues, he stepped into a world that showed little tolerance for a Hispanic who spoke only a little bit of English and was not familiar with American culture. Clemente's fierce pride and burning desire to excel enabled him to overcome such racial prejudice. He was always at his best when he was faced with a challenge.

Despite the rough treatment Clemente encountered, he always made it a point to give as much as he could, both on the field and off, to the game he loved. On one occasion, a shopkeeper refused to let Clemente pay for an item he wanted to purchase. When he was a boy, the shopkeeper said, he had gone to a game at Forbes Field and had sat in the right-field stands. During the game, a foul ball came his way. He grabbed it excitedly, only to have another fan wrestle it away from him.

Between innings, Clemente had come over to the stands and had given him another ball. The new ball was, the right fielder had explained, "for the one they took away from you."

"That's why I can't charge you," the shopkeeper concluded.

No other Latin American player before Clemente had attained such popularity. That is not surprising, for he often went out of his way to satisfy his fans. Every year, after the Pirates ended their season, he would return to Puerto Rico and play on a local Winter League team so his hometown fans could watch him play in person.

"A country without idols is nothing," Clemente insisted. "I send out 20,000 autographed pictures a year to the kids. I feel proud when a kid asks me for my autograph....I believe we owe something to the people who watch us. They work hard for their money."

And so Roberto Clemente worked hard, too, and became a superstar both on and off the field.

2

"EARN IT"

Roberto Walker Clemente was born on August 18, 1934, in Carolina, a city in northeast Puerto Rico. He had a sister and three brothers, as well as a step-sister and step-brother, and they all lived with Melchor and Luisa Clemente in a wooden frame house in a section of Carolina known as San Antón.

The area that surrounded San Antón was made up mostly of acres of sugar cane. Roberto's father, Melchor, supported his large family by working in the sugar cane fields for the Rubert Brothers Sugar Company. After helping to harvest the crop, he would load it and ship it off to the mills, where it was processed into sugar.

Cutting down sugar cane in the hot Caribbean sun was hard work that did not pay very well. Melchor earned two dollars a week at the job; when he finally became a foreman, he saw his salary rise to four dollars a week. But there was not much he could do about making so little money. Except for sugar cane, San Antón did not have any other industry.

Roberto attended elementary school in a small

Clemente first played in the Puerto Rican Winter Leagues during the 1952–53 season and, with the exception of 4 years, he played every winter through 1970–71. His Winter League batting average was .323, 6 points higher than his .317 major-league average.

classroom, and he learned his lessons well. He was a quiet, respectful boy who always listened to his elders and did what he was told.

When Roberto was nine years old, he asked his father for a bicycle.

"Earn it," his father told him.

Roberto did. At six o'clock every morning, he carried a neighbor's empty milk can a half mile to the local grocery store. After the can was filled up, he lugged it back to the neighbor's house. He earned a few pennies a day for his labor and kept at it for three years. Finally, when he was 12 years old, he had saved up enough money to purchase a used bicycle.

This kind of manual labor helped Roberto develop into a powerfully built teenager. A sports lover, he liked to carry a rubber ball wherever he went and squeeze it to strengthen his hands. "Many times at night," he said in recalling his youth, "I lay in bed and threw the ball against the ceiling and caught it. Baseball was my whole life."

Occasionally, Roberto went on some errands that took him past Sixto Escobar Stadium in Puerto Rico's capital city of San Juan. Black baseball stars from the Negro Leagues in the United States often played there in the winter. Before long, Roberto became so attached to one of the players, future New York Giants star Monte Irvin, that Roberto's friends began to call the young Clemente "Monte Irvin."

Roberto's first big break came when he was 14 years old. He was playing ball with some friends on a sandlot when Roberto Marín, who was scouting players for his company's softball team, happened to stop by. Marín wasted little time in enlisting Clemente to play on the Sello

Rojo rice company team. "I never saw a boy who loved baseball like he did," Marín recalled.

Roberto started out as a shortstop, which was the same position he played for the Julio Vizcarrondo High School baseball team. Eventually, he proved to be better suited for the outfield and was moved to right field.

By the time Roberto was 16, his play had caused such a sensation at a San Juan softball tournament that he was invited to join the Juncos in the Puerto Rican Double-A League. The players in this baseball league were good enough to be scouted by major league clubs.

Marín, sensing just how much potential

Negro League star Monte Irvin, Clemente's boyhood hero, was a 30-year-old rookie when he finally got the chance to play in the major leagues. Irvin led the Puerto Rican Winter League in hitting in 1945–46 with a .389 average, and led the Negro Leagues in batting in both 1940 and 1941.

Roberto had as a ballplayer, approached Pedrín Zorilla, owner of the Santurce Crabbers, a team in Puerto Rico's Winter League. Marín told Zorilla, one of Puerto Rico's most respected baseball men and a part-time scout for the Brooklyn Dodgers, that he might want to sign up Clemente for the Crabbers. In their off season, players from both the Negro Leagues and the major leagues often joined teams in the Winter League, where the level of competition was only a notch or two below that of big-league action.

Zorilla first balked at Marín's glowing reports about Clemente and passed up several trips to see him play. Finally, Zorilla saw Roberto play in an exhibition game. Clemente banged out a long triple and two doubles and impressed as well with an eye-popping throw that nailed an opposing runner at third.

The part-time scout immediately recognized his own good fortune. Right after the game, he offered Clemente a Winter League contract for a reported $400 signing bonus and $45 a week. Still under the legal age, Roberto could only be signed up with his father's approval. Melchor Clemente held out for a slightly better deal, and the Santurce club finally agreed to pay Roberto a $500 bonus, a $60 weekly salary, and to give him a spanking new fielder's mitt.

The days that Clemente spent with the Santurce Crabbers were certainly not ones of limitless success and joy. They were the first test of patience for a rising young star who would constantly meet frustration and rejection along the rocky road to major league stardom. Santurce was fighting for a league championship, and Zorilla did not want to risk losing a game with an untried rookie. He was unwilling to insert an 18-

year-old fresh from an amateur league into a lineup boasting not only the New York Giants' young star Willie Mays but outfielders such as Bob Thurman and Willard Brown, two of the big leagues' first black ballplayers.

Clemente silently fumed at having to sit on the bench during his first season. His friend and earliest coach Roberto Marín had to persuade him not to quit on several different occasions.

When Clemente did play, he performed brilliantly. In one game late in the season, the Crabbers loaded the bases with two outs. Down two runs, this was their chance to tie or go ahead in the game. Bob Thurman was the batter, but he had trouble hitting lefthanded pitchers. The manager, Buster Clarkson, a veteran of the Negro Leagues, called Thurman back from the on-deck circle. Looking down the bench at Clemente, he called out, "Grab yourself a bat." Clemente bolted up the dugout steps and strode to the plate. The first pitch was a fastball, and Roberto swung and missed. Setting himself, he waited for the next pitch. Another fastball blazed in, but this time Clemente was ready. He swung and connected, lacing a line drive over the first baseman's head. Rounding first, Clemente raced to second, just sliding under the tag for a double. Three runs had scored, and Santurce had the lead.

From that game on, Clemente played more and more. The following year, his second season with the Santurce Crabbers, Clemente was a starter. He dazzled the fans with great catches in the outfield and batted leadoff. He ended the year with a .288 batting average and had proved to all observers that he was ready for the professional leagues in the United States.

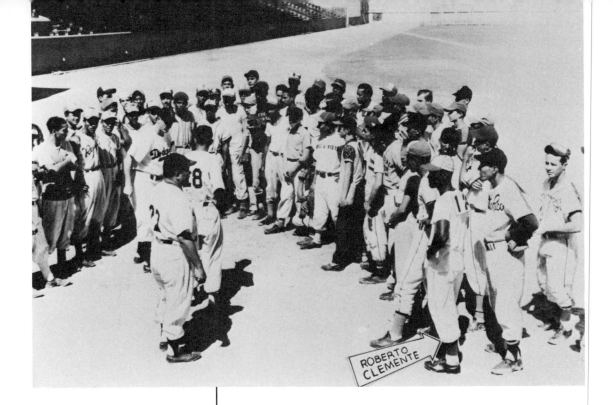

ROBERTO CLEMENTE

The Santurce Crabbers and the Brooklyn Dodgers held a baseball clinic together in 1952. It was at this clinic that Clemente (in lower right) was spotted by Dodger scouts.

Big-league scouts were not long in beating a path to his door. Most ardent in their pursuit were the Dodgers and the Giants, followed closely by the Milwaukee Braves, the St. Louis Cardinals, and the New York Yankees. Zorilla—perhaps inspired by visions of Mays and Clemente remaining in the same outfield in the major leagues—quietly urged Giants owner Horace Stoneham to bid for the youngster. Stoneham refused, saying his scouts had told him that Clemente would strike out too much against big-league pitching.

Dodgers scouting director Al Campanis had done his homework more thoroughly, however. He rushed in to offer a $10,000 signing bonus. No Hispanic player had ever been offered such a large bonus before. Future Hall of Famer Juan Marichal, from the Dominican Republic, would be given only $500 to sign with the Giants several years later.

Clemente discussed the offer with Señor Zorilla. It was a fair deal, and the Dodgers were a powerhouse in the National League. Zorilla advised Clemente that it was a good offer. After thinking it over for a few minutes, Clemente told Zorilla to tell the Dodgers that he would sign the contract.

Then, a few hours later, a Milwaukee Braves scout contacted Clemente and offered him a bonus of $28,000. The Braves had finished a surprising second behind the Dodgers in 1953 and were eager to pair the talents of Clemente with those of another young player, Hank Aaron, who had hit .362 in the minor leagues in 1953. But Roberto had committed himself to the Brooklyn Dodgers, and there was no looking back. Like his father, Roberto was always a man of his word.

3

A SLOW START

Roberto Clemente joined the Brooklyn Dodgers' top minor league club, the Montreal Royals, in the spring of 1954. The young Puerto Rican star was determined to play on an every-day basis and earn a promotion to the major leagues. The Dodgers, however, had no intention of playing their raw recruit regularly in Montreal.

According to the rules at the time, by signing Clemente to a bonus of more than $4,000 and then sending him directly to the minors, the Dodgers had to promote him to their major league roster by the end of his rookie campaign. Otherwise, he could be claimed at the end of the season by another major league club.

Brooklyn wanted to hold on to Clemente but did not foresee having an open space for him on its 1955 roster. The club already had three top-flight outfielders: future Hall of Famer Duke Snider, 1953 National League batting champion Carl Furillo, and a promising youngster named Sandy Amoros. So they came up with a plan without telling Clemente about it. They attempted to hold on to him by keeping him from playing.

Clemente makes a sensational catch against Bobby Thomson of the Cubs in 1958.

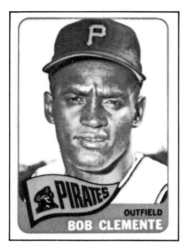

Clemente's 1965 Topps card.

The Dodgers hoped that the other teams, without much of a chance to see him perform, would decide not to draft him at the end of the season.

If some other ball club did decide to draft Clemente, the Dodgers hoped it would be a team that selected ahead of Brooklyn's arch rivals, the New York Giants. "We didn't want the Giants to have Clemente and Willie Mays in the same outfield," Dodgers vice-president Buzzie Bavasi admitted.

Clemente got into only 87 Royals games in 1954 and hit .257. In many of those, his role was limited to late-inning, pinch-hitting stints and brief appearances as a defensive replacement. "If I struck out, I stayed in the lineup," he recalled. "If I played well, I was benched."

Nevertheless, Pittsburgh's superscout Clyde Sukeforth and general manager Branch Rickey, both of whom had been with the Dodgers organization, had heard of the young prospect. When the two had been with the Dodgers, it was Branch Rickey who had assigned Sukeforth to scout Jackie Robinson in the Negro Leagues and the two had eventually brought the young star to the Dodgers. One day in 1954, Rickey sent Sukeforth to scout a sore-armed pitcher named Joe Black, the 1952 National League Rookie of the Year, who had recently been sent down to Montreal to try and work his arm back in shape. Sukeforth took one look at Clemente during the pregame workout and became convinced that *he* was the player to go after.

"You and I will never live long enough to draft a boy with this kind of ability for $4,000 again," Sukeforth told Rickey. "This is something that happens once in a lifetime." Rickey pondered a moment. "Keep an eye on him, Clyde."

Another Pirates official, Howie Haak, a veteran "bird dog" who recruited Latin American players, was assigned to watch Clemente perform. In two weeks Haak only saw Clemente bat four times. Clemente, as frustrated with Montreal as he was his first year with Santurce, almost left the team. Haak talked Roberto into not quitting the Royals. Haak explained to Clemente that if he were to leave the Montreal team, the Dodgers would be able to hold on to his contract for yet another season. That would cause him to miss out on his chance to play regularly in the majors with the Pirates, who were eager to land him.

Sukeforth took one last trip to watch Clemente perform. Although Roberto was kept on the bench, Sukeforth talked with the Royals manager, Max Macon, about him. "Max, do me a favor. I want you to take care of our boy Clemente. Just look after him as you would your own boy. Protect him for us, Max, because he's just as good as ours."

Macon laughed. "You mean you want *him*?"

Sukeforth thought Macon was trying to throw him off the trail. "Do me a favor, Max." Sukeforth knew that the Dodgers would not protect Clemente by putting him on their major league roster, and that the last team in the National League would get the first pick in the annual winter draft of bonus players. And the Pirates were well on their way to locking up a last-place finish, 11 games behind the seventh-place Chicago Cubs.

Finally, on November 22, 1954, the Pirates selected Roberto Clemente.

Roberto's good fortune was marred by personal tragedy a month later. His oldest brother, Luis, died from a brain tumor on New Year's Eve.

Roberto had visited his dying brother's bed-side for the first time in the months shortly after the 1954 baseball season. As Roberto left the hospital that day, his car was struck broadside, at 60 miles hour, by another automobile with a drunken driver at the wheel. Clemente miracu-lously escaped this near-fatal accident, but he suffered severe and persistent spinal damage that would haunt him for the remainder of his career.

When Clemente joined the Pirates in 1955, they were the worst team in the National League. The Bucs—short for buccaneers, or pirates—had lost more than 100 games in each of the past three seasons.

Pittsburgh would not perform much better in 1955. They posted a record of 60 and 94 and finished in last place for the fourth year in a row.

The Pirates were gearing up for better days, however. Along with good-fielding shortstop Dick Groat, returning after two years in the army, and outfield slugger Frank Thomas, the team had three excellent pitchers in Elroy Face, Bob Friend, and Vernon Law. Second baseman Bill Mazeroski was in the minors and would join the parent club the following year. And, beginning in 1955, they had Roberto Clemente.

The rookie right fielder hit only .255 that season. As exciting as his free-swinging style was for the fans, it proved to be a constant source of worry for the Pirates' brain trust. The Bucs had their batting instructor, Hall of Famer George Sisler, work with Clemente to improve his ap-proach to hitting. Sisler proved to be a good teacher. Clemente became a more selective bat-ter during his sophomore campaign and saw his average climb to .311.

Roberto's stellar second season was followed by a disastrous, injury-plagued third campaign, however. His batting average dropped to .253, and he drove in only 30 runs. At times, he showed flashes of brilliance. But he did not seem to belong in the same class as former Winter-League teammate Willie Mays, or his boyhood hero, Monte Irvin. At the end of three seasons, Roberto Clemente was anything but an established big-league star.

The Pirates barely escaped the cellar in 1956, and in 1957 they tied the equally hapless Chicago Cubs for dead last. These years saw the Pittsburgh team hire manager after manager. First, there was veteran Fred Haney. Next came Bobby Bragan for a slightly longer spell. Finally, stability arrived in the person of Danny Murtaugh, who became manager 104 games into the 1957 campaign.

The losing and the accompanying turmoil were not easy for the extremely competitive

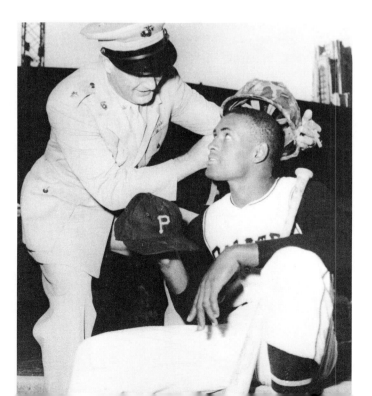

In 1958, Clemente trades his Pirates cap for an army combat helmet. Major Lutner Reedy of the 12th Infantry Battalion fits the army helmet on the Pirate outfielder.

Forbes Field, named after a general who fought in the French and Indian War, was opened on June 30, 1909. On June 28, 1970, the last Pirates game was played there. The stadium was never known as a home-run park but was renown for three baggers. In the 62 seasons the Pirates played in Forbes Field, they led the N.L. in triples 33 times.

Clemente to bear. And his injured lower back, which limited him to playing in only 111 games in 1957, did not make matters any easier. "I told my mother and father," he recalled, "'I will try it for one more year. If I still hurt, then I quit.'"

At the conclusion of the 1957 season, Clemente received what turned out to be a lucky break. He was called to serve in the U.S. military and spent the next six months with the Marines. This stint in the military allowed his back to mend somewhat.

When the 1958 baseball campaign got under way, Clemente was ready to climb the road to stardom. He hit .289 for the season and collected 40 extra-base hits. Although he was powerfully built, Roberto did not try to be a home-run hitter. He realized that he would have to adjust his batting style to take advantage of the Pirates' spacious home park: "When I first saw Forbes Field, I said, 'Forget home runs.' I was strong, but nobody is that strong. I became a line-drive hitter."

Just as Clemente began to improve, so did the Pirates. In one of the tightest pennant races in league history, the inspired Pittsburgh team, led by All-Stars Bill Mazeroski, Frank Thomas, Bob Friend, and outfielder Bob Skinner battled it out with the San Francisco Giants and Milwaukee Braves. The talented Braves finally prevailed, but the Bucs finished solidly in second place, a pennant contender for the first time in many seasons.

Despite his team's success, Clemente experienced a major setback during the season. In an April 30th game against Los Angeles, his snap throw from deep in the outfield brought immediate pain to his right arm. Suddenly, a new injury was born. For the next several seasons, Roberto threw hard only when he had to.

In spite of this injury, Roberto remained in the lineup for 140 games during the 1958 season. Perhaps he was inspired by the Bucs' sudden and unexpected success. Whatever the reason, his continuously sore arm did not prevent him from throwing accurately enough to record a league-leading 22 outfield assists.

Pirate fans were looking forward to 1959, and many hoped there might be a National League pennant flying over old Forbes Field. Clemente and the other Pirates shared their hopes. But on May 2nd, Clemente was hit on the right elbow by a pitch and, one week later, was placed on the 40-day disabled list. He appeared in just 105 games in 1959, one of the lowest totals of his career, and he drove in only 50 runs. As the 1950s were closing out, Clemente had yet to hit more than 7 home runs or drive in more than 60 runs; only once had he topped the .300 mark. But the 1960s would show the baseball world what a marvelous ballplayer Roberto Clemente could be.

4

THE UNSUNG ALL-STAR

Major league baseball in the late 1950s featured a number of fence-busting sluggers and flawless flychasers, including Willie Mays, Mickey Mantle, Duke Snider, Stan Musial, and Hank Aaron. But none of them displayed more flash than the young and strong-armed Puerto Rican outfielder who performed so valiantly for Pittsburgh. Clemente was a major factor in reviving the Pirates.

The few headlines that came Clemente's way during his earliest seasons did not quite measure up to what this proud ballplayer had hoped for. He was a hero in Puerto Rico but not on the mainland United States.

One day in New York City, Clemente went shopping for some furniture. A salesperson took him aside and began to show Roberto some items that were less expensive than the ones he had first looked at. When he asked why, the salesman replied, "Well, you don't have enough money to buy that."

The ballplayer promptly took out a thick wad of bills and waved them in the air. The salesman

Clemente bangs into the outfield wall at Chicago's Wrigley Field trying to catch Jim Hickman's triple.

immediately apologized, adding that he thought Clemente was "just another Puerto Rican."

Naturally, Clemente was upset by his encounters with racial prejudice. "Hispanic players," he once said to a white sportswriter, "need time to get adjusted here like you would need time to get adjusted in our countries. We lead different lives in the United States. We're always meeting new people, seeing new faces. Everything is strange. The language barrier is great at first."

By 1960, however, Clemente was well on his way to separating his off-the-field difficulties from his actions on the field. It was a banner year for the Pirates and everyone associated with the team. After a near miss at the pennant in 1958 and a fourth-place finish the following year, the 1960 Pirates accomplished nothing short of a miracle. They won the National League pennant

Bill Mazeroski is mobbed at home plate after breaking a 9–9 tie with his ninth-inning homer in game 7 of the 1960 World Series.

for the first time in 33 years.

Clemente played a major role in helping Pittsburgh finish the season with a 95 and 59 record, seven games in front of Milwaukee. He recorded the Bucs' second-best batting average, .314, and was second in home runs with 16. He led the squad in runs batted in with 94.

Clemente also continued to shine brilliantly on defense, again pacing the circuit in assists for outfielders (19) and repeatedly making spectacular plays that turned near-losses into miraculous victories. During one stretch of the season, he had to spend five days in a hospital after crashing into a wall while making a game-saving catch of a drive hit by Willie Mays.

Yet Clemente's brilliant play often seemed to go unnoticed. Because the team had constantly posted a poor record, the Pirates did not draw much media attention. In fact, Clemente had the opportunity to showcase his talent to a large audience only when he played in a World Series.

Clemente made his first World Series appearance in 1960 and did not disappoint any of his fans. He batted .310 against the powerhouse New York Yankees, fielded flawlessly, and hit safely in every game. After six games, the underdog Pirates were tied with the highly favored Yankees at three games apiece, even though the Bucs had been outscored by 29 runs.

In game 7, Bill Mazeroski, who batted .320 for the series, hit a dramatic home run in the ninth inning to win the game and give the Pirates the championship. The city of Pittsburgh deliriously celebrated its first world title since 1925. Clemente left the Pirates' locker room to join the thousands of fans cheering wildly in the streets.

After the Series victory, Roberto returned to

his native Puerto Rico, where he soon suffered a major disappointment. He regarded himself as a leading candidate to win the league's Most Valuable Player Award, and he badly wanted to win this honor. To receive the award would indicate to him that he had been accepted by the American public.

When the voting was revealed for the Most Valuable Player Award, Roberto's Pittsburgh teammate Dick Groat was a runaway winner. Groat had led the league in batting, posting a .325 average, but he had only hit 2 homers and knocked in 50 runs. Fellow Pirate Don Hoak, who had played brilliantly in the infield but hit only .282, was an even bigger surprise as the second-leading vote-getter. That Clemente was way down the list in eighth place was the biggest shock of all.

What hurt Clemente was not so much that he had not won the award. Far more disappointing to the proud Pirate as he read the results of the sportswriters' tally in the local San Juan press was that he had received so few votes and had finished so far out of the running.

Roberto's reaction was to return to the baseball wars in Pittsburgh with a renewed dedication and determination. He would make the fans and press sit up and take notice if it was the last thing he did, and at whatever the cost to his injury-prone and already battered body.

What followed was the most brilliant stretch of Roberto's career. In 1961, he established himself as a true superstar. His average soared to .351, and he became the first Latin American ever to capture a National League batting crown. He hit 23 homers, scored 100 runs, and knocked out more than 200 hits for the first time in his

League president Warren Giles presents Clemente with a silver bat for winning the 1965 N.L. batting title. Clemente collected four of these bats during his career.

career. He finished among the league leaders in hits (seven behind the pacesetter, Cincinnati's Vada Pinson) and total bases (where he stood fifth). Although the Pirates sagged badly to a sixth-place finish in 1961, it was through no lack of effort by Clemente, who was voted to the National League All-Star team for the first time.

Clemente, hitting .357 at the break, performed well in the All-Star game in San Francisco's Candlestick Park. He hit a first inning triple and scored the first run. The National League had a comfortable 3–1 lead after eight innings when suddenly a windstorm blew up. The swirling wind was so bad that the National League committed three errors in the top of the ninth. Pitcher Stu Miller was blown off the mound and a balk was called on the play, advancing two runners and allowing the American League to tie the game up. In the tenth inning, Clemente came up with the score tied and Willie Mays and Frank

Three future Hall of Famers pose after their All-Star game heroics in 1961: (left to right) Clemente, Willie Mays and Hank Aaron.

Robinson on base. The pitcher was knuckleballer Hoyt Wilhelm, who was tough to hit even when the wind was not blowing. Clemente waited on the pitch and drove it hard into right field. A delighted Mays raced to the plate clapping his hands all the way.

Afterward, the reporters crowded around Mays to ask him about his double and game-winning run. "I didn't do it," Mays replied and gestured toward Clemente. "This man next to me did it." Even if Clemente's brilliance was still a secret to some fans, Mays and the other players knew how good he was. Clemente's Pirate manager, Danny Murtaugh, also appreciated his skills. Murtaugh, as All-Star manager, had allowed Clemente to play the entire game, even though Henry Aaron was sitting on the bench.

From 1959 through 1962, there were two All-Star games played. Clemente was hitless in the second game of 1961, but in the 1962 classic in Washington, D.C., he had 3 hits in 3 at-bats to help the National League pull even with the American League in All-Star wins.

Following Clemente's 1961 offensive explosion came six consecutive seasons in which he batted over .300. In fact, he topped that mark in 12 of his last 13 seasons. He won the batting title in 1964, hitting a robust .339, but the Pirates finished tied for sixth in the 10-team National League. On the first of October, manager Danny Murtaugh resigned because of health reasons, and Harry Walker was named as his replacement. Murtaugh would return as interim manager in 1967, and again as permanent manager in 1970.

Clemente repeated as batting champion in 1965, with a .329 average, and the Pirates improved to finish third. In 1966, his Pirate teammate Matty Alou won the batting title as Clemente finished fourth, with a .317 average. The Dodgers, with stronger pitching than the Pirates, finished three games ahead of Pittsburgh and a game and a half up on San Francisco.

Despite the Pirates' third-place finish, the 1966 season saw Roberto finally get the recognition that he deserved. Due in part to his hitting 29 homers, batting in 119 runs, and scoring 105, he was named the National League's Most Valuable Player. The Pirates, recognizing the all-around abilities of their great star, rewarded Clemente with a $100,000 contract, the first ever in Pittsburgh history. He joined five other stars who were earning $100,000 or more: Willie Mays, Hank Aaron, Mickey Mantle, and Frank Robinson. "The best right fielder in the business," observed Pirates general manager Joe L. Brown of the Pirate star.

5

PERSONAL TRIUMPHS

$\mathbf{O}$ne day in the winter of 1963, Roberto Clemente was standing in a drugstore in his hometown of Carolina when he noticed a tall, attractive young woman. The 29-year-old ballplayer found out that her name was Vera Cristina Zabala and that she worked in a nearby bank. Roberto went home and, before he had spoken even one word to Vera, told his mother he had found the woman he was going to marry.

Things did not go according to plan, however. The first time Clemente tried to telephone her, she refused to speak to him. "My family was raised like the old times," Vera explained later. "We had to ask permission to go from here to the corner."

Several weeks later, Vera finally agreed to go on a date with Roberto, so long as they were accompanied by a chaperone. During their first meeting, Clemente discovered that Vera had no idea that he was Puerto Rico's most famous

Batting against the Mets on September 20, 1970, Clemente hits a pop foul and grimaces in pain. Catcher Jerry Grote watches the ball. This play aggravated Clemente's back pain, and he played little for the remainder of the season.

athlete. But she quickly found out on the day that he visited her at the bank. Everyone in the building mobbed the visiting star.

A year later, Roberto and Vera were married. They moved into a new house in a wealthy section of Río Piedras and soon started a family. They had three boys: Roberto, Jr., Luis, and Enrique.

Everyone in Puerto Rico idolized Roberto. But baseball fans in the United States generally regarded him in one of two ways.

In the eyes of some people, the Pirates' right fielder was a dazzling ballplayer who would swing at any pitch near the plate and then run the base paths with reckless abandon. One of the most exciting plays in baseball is that of a batter connecting for a triple, an extra-base hit that combines a special blend of foot speed, daring, and raw power. The three-base hit was Clemente's trademark. He reached double figures in triples during nine different seasons, including six in a row between the years 1965 and 1970.

According to other people, Clemente's exciting style of play was overshadowed by his reputation as a malingerer—someone who fakes injury and shows little desire to play hard. But Roberto's injuries were certainly real enough. Few players have performed with as much pain over the course of a career that spanned nearly 2,500 big-league games. Yet Clemente was routinely criticized for faking injury.

Whenever the Pirates right fielder returned to the lineup after sitting out a few games to nurse an injury, he would play well, as he always did. That made some people wonder: If he's playing so well, he could not have been hurt.

Perhaps it was Clemente's openness with

Roberto kisses his bride, Vera, after their marriage in a Catholic church near San Juan on November 14, 1964.

management and the press that contributed to this negative image. He let people know when he was injured—and wound up getting criticized for not playing hurt, like some other athletes did.

Roberto tried to shrug off this negative image. While the Pirates followed their 1960 World Championship season by finishing sixth, fourth, eighth, and then sixth again, Clemente simply tore up the league. Still, because the Pirates went immediately from world champs to also-rans, the blame had to fall somewhere. Often, it fell on Roberto.

Throughout all the frustrations of the Pirates' up-and-down seasons in the 1960s, Clemente chafed most especially at a nickname his teammates gave him. His anger at receiving almost no notice among sportswriters in the 1960 MVP balloting prompted his fellow Pirates to call him "No Votes." The nickname, however, inspired Clemente to try that much harder.

Roberto always took great pride in himself and his Puerto Rican heritage. His father had

Clemente slides safely into third against the Cubs as Ron Santo takes a late throw. During his 18 years in a Bucs uniform, Clemente led the N.L. in triples 12 times.

taught him to think like that. One day, when Roberto was still a youngster, a passing car carrying plantation owner Don Pepito Rubert passed by. Melchor Clemente told his son, "He is no better than you." It was a lesson the youngster never forgot.

By the spring of 1970, the years of playing baseball in the summer in the United States and Winter League ball in Puerto Rico had taken its toll. "I need rest," Roberto Clemente stated, "I almost quit last year. My shoulder was hurting. I started feeling a little better, but the ache in my shoulder is still there." Sure enough, injuries throughout the 1970 season cut his game appearances to 108 and his at-bats to 412, the fewest of any big-league season except for his last. Nevertheless, he hit a resounding .352.

The thrill of a pennant race helped to keep Clemente going.

Best of all, when the Pirates played their very first game in brand new Three Rivers Stadium in mid-July, the occasion was designated by club officials as "Roberto Clemente Night." During the evening's festivities, Clemente was presented with a scroll several yards in length. It contained the signatures and good wishes of more than 300,000 Puerto Ricans.

A tight National League East division title race saw the Pirates pull away from both the Chicago Cubs and the New York Mets in the season's waning days. A red-hot Clemente led the way. On August 22, he had five hits in a 16-inning 2–1 victory over the Dodgers. He followed that up the next night with another five hits as the Pirates won, 11–0. Two successive five-hit games was a feat that no other player in major-league history had ever accomplished.

However, the sweet summer of 1970 came to a disappointing end in the autumn. Pittsburgh won the Eastern Division with an 89 and 73 record, as the Cubs again finished in second place. But then a powerful Cincinnati Reds team, which featured Pete Rose, Johnny Bench, and Cuban standout Tony Perez in its "Big Red Machine" lineup, swept the Pirates in three games in the playoffs. Clemente batted just .214 for the short series, with only three singles and a single run scored in 14 plate appearances. It was to be the worst post-season performance of his career.

6

PLAYING TO WIN

W hen the 1971 campaign began, Clemente was determined to lead his team to another World Series title. In a key game against the Houston Astros, he made a game-saving catch while crashing into the unpadded cement wall in the right-field corner. "When I play baseball," Clemente explained, "I don't play easy one day and hard the next."

Unlike the previous season, the Pirates did not engage in a tight race. They won their division easily, by a margin of seven games, finishing with a record of 97 and 65.

A healthy Clemente appeared in 132 games and performed brilliantly once more on the field and at the plate. He batted .341, clubbed in 86 runs, and made only two errors. His teammates Dock Ellis, Manny Sanguillen, and future Hall of Famer Willie Stargell were the other key contributors to the Bucs' winning season.

Clemente had started the season slowly, as

In game 6 of the 1971 World Series, Clemente connects for a home run against Baltimore's Jim Palmer. In his previous at-bat, he had hit a triple.

45

he often did. But as the year wore on, it was apparent that he was a man on a mission. He still had not fulfilled his dream of showcasing his talent to the world.

Clemente had told a reporter in the late 1960s, "I believe I can hit with anybody in baseball. Maybe I can't hit with the power of a Mays or a Frank Robinson or a Hank Aaron, but I can hit."

In the All-Star game on July 13, Clemente showed his power when he crashed a home run for the National League. Four days later, the Pirates beat the San Diego Padres in a 17-inning marathon when Clemente hit another homer.

Clemente kept on hitting right through the National League playoff series against the San Francisco Giants. He hit .333 as the Pirates won the series in four games.

The 1971 World Series will always be remembered as the time when Roberto Clemente finally received the respect he had deserved for so many years. Rarely has a fall classic served as a better showcase of a single player. Clemente dominated the action both offensively and defensively.

The Pirates were underdogs to the powerful Baltimore Orioles heading into the Series . The Orioles had won more than a hundred games three years in a row, and in 1971 they featured a pitching staff with four 20-game winners. No pitching quartet had done that since the 1920 White Sox. Feisty Orioles manager Earl Weaver told reporters, "I've got the best ball club in the universe. Great spirit. Great ability. Great everything. We'll beat these Pirates. Not easy, but we'll beat them."

After the first two games, it looked like Weaver was right. The Baltimore Orioles, opening the

Series at home, swept the Bucs, 5–3 and 11–3. Clemente played well, at one point uncorking an outfield throw that Baltimore catcher Andy Etchebarren called "the greatest throw I ever saw by an outfielder." But it was not enough to put the Pirates on top.

When Pittsburgh returned home for game 3, Clemente spurred the team's comeback effort. They won the next three games to take an edge in the Series, three games to two.

In game 6, Clemente hit a triple and a home run, which meant that he had gotten at least 1 hit in all 13 of his World Series games. Baltimore, however, won the contest in the 10th inning, 3–2, on a Brooks Robinson sacrifice fly. As in their previous World Series appearance, Pittsburgh would have to play the full seven games.

Roberto Clemente was not about to be denied. In game 7, he smacked a home run in the fourth

Eight days after Three Rivers Stadium opened on July 16, 1970, 43,000 fans crowded in for Roberto Clemente Night. Hundreds of fans travelled from San Juan to attend the festivities and thousands more watched the ceremony on television in Puerto Rico.

inning to put his team in the lead. The round-tripper helped provide the final margin of victory as the Bucs scored again in the eighth to win, 2–1, and take the World Championship. The Pirates became just the sixth team in baseball history to win a World Series after losing the first two games. After the last game, Brooks Robinson, the peerless third baseman for the Orioles, just shook his head when asked about Clemente. "You read about him, you hear about him, but in real life he's even better."

Clemente's numbers for the 1971 World Series were phenomenal. He hit at a .414 clip, registering 12 hits along with 2 homers and 4 crucial RBIs. He fielded flawlessly, handling 15 outfield chances with his customary flare. This time around, he was the unanimous choice to receive the sports car presented by *Sport* magazine in

Umpire Doug Harvey presents Roberto with the ball he connected with for his 3,000th major-league hit.

honor of his being named the Series MVP.

At long last, the Pirates, after a full decade, had won another World Championship flag. But this time the entire nation had been watching on television while Clemente performed his heroics, for this World Series marked the first time in baseball history that a Series game had been played at night. According to NBC, the game was seen on half the television sets in the country.

Clemente's all-around play had finally won him widespread attention. "It was," said writer Roger Angell, "a kind of baseball that none of us had ever seen before—throwing and running and hitting at something close to the level of absolute perfection, playing to win but also playing the game as if it were a form of punishment for everyone else on the field."

With a veteran lineup, Pittsburgh easily repeated as division champions in 1972, winning the title by 11 games over the Chicago Cubs. Clemente finished the year with a .312 batting average.

While the Pirates were running away with the division, attention turned toward Clemente's chase for his 3,000th hit. His 2,999th hit came against Steve Carlton in Philadelphia, and Clemente hoped to get his 3,000th in front of his fans in Pittsburgh. The Pirates returned home to face Tom Seaver of the Mets on a cold and rainy evening.

Clemente stepped in against the Mets ace in the first inning and chopped a ball that struck Seaver's glove and bounded to the second baseman. The second baseman hurried to make the play, and the ball bounced off of his glove as well. With Clemente safe at first, all eyes looked to the scoreboard to see what the call was. When

After the 1972 season ended, Roberto talked with Puerto Rican youngsters during the filming of a commercial at Three Rivers Stadium.

"H" for hit flashed up, all 24,000 fans roared their approval. Time was called, and the first baseman presented the ball to Clemente. Suddenly, the "H" disappeared on the scoreboard and was replaced by an "E" for error. The cheers turned to groans. In his following at-bats against Seaver, Clemente went hitless.

The next afternoon was the last day of the regular season and Clemente's last chance in the 1972 season to get his 3,000th. Pitching for the Mets was a young lefthander, Jon Matlack. In the first inning, Roberto struck out. His next at-bat came in the fourth inning. The first pitch was a fastball for a strike, and then Matlack came in with a curve. Clemente leaned over the plate and stroked the ball on a line to left center. This time there was no doubt it was a hit. As Clemente stood on second base, time was called to present him with the ball. Clemente waved to the crowd, acknowledging the cheers. It was a very special moment for Roberto, because only 10 other men had ever gotten as many base hits.

The 1972 playoff series against Cincinnati proved to be anticlimactic. The Reds eked out a three-games-to-two victory, nipping the Pirates, 4–3, with a ninth-inning rally in the final contest. The Bucs lost the pennant on a wild pitch, as their usually reliable pitcher Bob Moose uncorked an errant fastball that allowed the winning run to score.

Like most of the Pirates, Clemente slumped badly in the 1972 playoffs. He collected only four hits—one of them a homer—and posted a meager .235 average. Although disappointed, Roberto did not dwell on his team's failure to return to the World Series. When he flew home to Puerto Rico after the National League playoffs, he had something other than baseball on his mind.

For a long time, Clemente had wanted to help build a large recreation complex in San Juan. As he envisioned it, the Sports City would be a place where youngsters could play to their hearts' delight.

7

A GREAT GLORY IS LOST

Most ballplayers who have been injured during the course of the year spend the off-season resting their battered body. In addition to his playing every year in the Winter League, Roberto Clemente's off-seasons were always filled with endless public service and personal appearances throughout his native island. Thus, when a devastating earthquake struck the Central American nation of Nicaragua on December 23, 1972, he sprang into action. Clemente hoped to make use of his status as a sports hero to gain support for a relief effort.

Clemente had been to Nicaragua's capital city of Managua a year earlier to manage the Puerto Rican national baseball team in the world amateur championships. Other than his brief visits there, he had very little connection with the people who lived in Nicaragua. Yet he felt a sense of kinship with all the citizens of Latin America, and he wanted to help those whose

Christmas Eve 1972, the morning after the disastrous earthquake in Managua, Nicaragua, finds smoke still rising from the ravaged city.

lives had been turned upside-down by the earth-quake.

Clemente became chairman of the Puerto Rican chapter of the Nicaraguan relief effort. At first, his role was to head a drive to elicit clothing, food, and money for the disaster victims. At one point, he even went door to door in his neighborhood to ask for donations.

Clemente then arranged to have the relief supplies stored in San Juan's Hiram Bithorn Stadium. Next, he chartered trucks to collect and transport the supplies to the stadium. When that was done, he chartered an airplane to fly the relief supplies across the Gulf of Mexico to the needy victims in Managua.

Roberto initially had no plans to go to Nicaragua with the supplies. But when reports began to reach Puerto Rico that some of the first shipments of earthquake aid had fallen into corrupt hands, he decided it was necessary for him to make sure the supplies were indeed delivered to the earthquake victims. "If I go to Nicaragua, the stealing will stop," he said. "They would not dare to steal from Roberto Clemente."

Clemente and four other people went to the airport to board an old DC-7 cargo plane bound for Nicaragua on the afternoon of December 31, 1972. By going on this mission, he would not be able to celebrate New Year's Eve with his family.

The aircraft, which was dangerously over-loaded, suffered several mechanical breakdowns that delayed the takeoff. Finally, at around nine o'clock in the evening, the plane roared down the airport runway. As soon as the DC-7 was airborne, though, it developed engine trouble. Unable to correct the problem, the pilot radioed to the control tower that he was going to turn the

A United States stamp honoring Clemente was issued in 1984 in Carolina, Puerto Rico.

plane around and bring it back to the airport for an emergency landing. The plane banked hard to the left and fell into the Atlantic Ocean a few miles from the San Juan shore. No one survived the crash.

The next morning, thousands of people went out on a rainy New Year's Day to watch the rescue operation. The inauguration of the new governor was canceled and three days of mourning were declared. Vera Clemente, along with many others, maintained a vigil along the Atlantic coast that lasted for days, until all hope of finding their hero was lost. The plane's tail section was finally located a week after the crash.

For the next 11 days, Coast Guard boats and aircraft searched for the remains of the flight's

In 1973, Mrs. Vera Clemente accepts her husband's plaque at the induction ceremonies at the Baseball Hall of Fame. In attendance are (left to right) fellow inductees Warren Spahn, Monte Irvin, George Kelly and Williams Evans, who represented his late grandfather, umpire Billy Evans. Baseball commissioner Bowie Kuhn holds the plaque.

Mrs. Roberto Clemente and her three sons listen to former Pirate general manager Joe Brown speak at the unveiling of the Clemente statue in front of Sports City in 1977.

passengers. Clemente's teammate Manny Sanguillen donned some scuba gear and searched on his own. A pair of eyeglasses, believed to be the pilot's, and a small black briefcase known to be Roberto's were all that was ever recovered. No bodies were ever found.

On January 4, 1973, a joint mass for Clemente was held simultaneously in a church in downtown Pittsburgh and in Carolina's San Fernando Church, where the fallen star had been baptized and married. "Our people," said the island's new governor, Rafael Hernandez Colón, "have lost one of their great glories."

Two months later, the Baseball Writers Association of America waived the usual five-year waiting period and gave Roberto Clemente the unprecedented honor of immediate induction into the Hall of Fame.

On Opening Day of the 1973 season, the Pittsburgh Pirates retired Clemente's uniform number, 21. Singer Ruth Fernandez, who had served with Clemente on the Nicaragua relief committee, sang the Puerto Rico anthem before the start of the game. "When you honor Roberto Clemente," she told the crowd, "you honor all Puerto Rico." Then the Pirates took the field for their game with the St. Louis Cardinals. With Manny Sanguillen playing Roberto's position in right field, the Pirates came from behind to defeat the Cards, 7–5.

Clemente's death spurred a large number of donations to his long standing dream of building a Sports City in Puerto Rico. Gradually, this dream became a reality on a grassy 600-acre site donated by the Puerto Rican government.

Today, Sports City stands proudly between Carolina and San Juan. There are six baseball fields, a batting cage, basketball courts, a swimming pool, tennis courts, and a dormitory. There is no admission charge to any youngster.

Roberto would be very pleased. Shortly before his death, he said of the sports complex: "It is the biggest ambition of my life....It will be open to everybody, no matter who they are....I will do this because this is what God meant me do to. Baseball is just something that gave me the chance to do this."

Sports City is a fitting monument to the memory of the island's first baseball Hall of Famer, Roberto Walker Clemente.

CHRONOLOGY

Aug. 18, 1934	Born Roberto Clemente Walker in Carolina, Puerto Rico (In the Spanish custom, Clemente was christened with his father's surname *Clemente* first, followed by his mother's surname, *Walker*)
Oct. 9, 1952	Signs first professional contract to play for the Santurce Crabbers in Puerto Rico's Winter League
Feb. 19, 1954	Signs with the Brooklyn Dodgers
Nov. 22, 1954	Pittsburgh Pirates select Clemente in the major-league draft of unprotected bonus prospects
Dec. 1954	Receives a spinal disc injury in an automobile accident
Dec. 31, 1954	Luis, Roberto's older brother, dies of a brain tumor
Oct. 13, 1960	Pirates capture World Series over the New York Yankees
Sept. 1961	Closes the season with a .351 batting average, and wins his first N.L. batting championship
Nov. 14, 1964	Marries Vera Cristina Zabala
Oct., 1966	Named National League Most Valuable Player
Sept. 1967	Wins his fourth and final league batting title with a .357 batting average
July 16, 1970	Pittsburgh's new Three Rivers Stadium is inaugurated with a special Roberto Clemente Night
Oct. 21, 1971	World Series MVP Clemente returns as a national hero to his native Puerto Rico after leading Pittsburgh to a dramatic comeback victory over the Baltimore Orioles
Jan. 29, 1972	Receives his twelfth Gold Glove Award
Sept. 30, 1972	Clemente's final base hit of the 1972 season and the last of his career is also his 3,000th
Dec. 31, 1972	Dies in plane crash off coast of San Juan, Puerto Rico, while flying supplies to earthquake victims of Nicaragua
Feb. 1972	Baseball Hall of Fame selection committee waives its normal five-year waiting rule and unanimously elects Clemente
April 6, 1973	Clemente's uniform number, 21, is retired

ROBERTO WALKER CLEMENTE
PITTSBURGH N. L. 1955-1972

MEMBER OF EXCLUSIVE 3,000-HIT CLUB. LED
NATIONAL LEAGUE IN BATTING FOUR TIMES.
HAD FOUR SEASONS WITH 200 OR MORE HITS
WHILE POSTING LIFETIME .317 AVERAGE AND
240 HOME RUNS. WON MOST VALUABLE PLAYER
AWARD 1966. RIFLE-ARMED DEFENSIVE STAR
SET N. L. MARK BY PACING OUTFIELDERS IN
ASSISTS FIVE YEARS. BATTED .362 IN TWO
WORLD SERIES, HITTING IN ALL 14 GAMES.

MAJOR LEAGUE STATISTICS

PITTSBURGH PIRATES

YEAR	TEAM	G	AB	R	H	2B	3B	HR	RBI	BA	SB
1955	PIT N	124	474	48	121	23	11	5	47	.255	2
1956		147	543	66	169	30	7	7	60	.311	6
1957		111	451	42	114	17	7	4	30	.253	0
1958		140	519	69	150	24	10	6	50	.289	8
1959		105	432	60	128	17	7	4	50	.296	2
1960		144	570	89	179	22	6	16	94	.314	4
1961		146	572	100	201	30	10	23	89	.351	4
1962		144	538	95	168	28	9	10	74	.312	6
1963		152	600	77	192	23	8	17	76	.320	12
1064		155	622	95	211	40	7	12	87	.339	5
1965		152	589	91	194	21	14	10	65	.329	8
1966		154	638	105	202	31	11	29	119	.317	7
1967		147	585	103	209	26	10	23	110	.357	9
1968		132	502	74	146	18	12	18	57	.291	2
1969		138	507	87	175	20	12	19	91	.345	4
1970		108	412	65	145	22	10	14	60	.352	3
1971		132	522	82	178	29	8	13	86	.341	1
1972		102	378	68	118	19	7	10	60	.312	0
Total		2433	9454	1416	3000	440	166	240	1305	.317	83
League Championship Series (3 years)		12	49	4	13	1	0	1	7	.265	0
World Series (2 years)		14	58	4	21	2	1	2	7	.362	0
All-Star Games (11 years)		14	31	3	10	2	1	0	4	.323	0

FURTHER READING

Bloomfield, Jerry. *Roberto Clemente, Pride of the Pirates.* Champaign, IL: Garrard Publishers, 1976.

Christine, Bill. *Roberto.* New York: Stadia Sports Publications, 1973.

Hano, Arnold. *Roberto Clemente, Batting King.* New York: G.P. Putnam, 1973.

Izenberg, Jerry. *Great Latin Sports Figures: The Proud People.* New York: Doubleday, 1976.

Kahn, Roger. *A Season in the Sun.* New York: Harper & Row, 1977.

Mercer, Charles E. *Roberto Clemente.* New York: G.P. Putnam, 1974.

Miller, Ira. *Roberto Clemente.* New York: Grosset & Dunlap, 1973.

Musick, Phil. *Who Was Roberto? A Biography of Roberto Clemente.* New York: Doubleday, 1974.

Newton, Clarke. *Famous Puerto Ricans.* New York: Dodd, Mead, 1975.

Olsen, Jack. *Roberto Clemente: The Great One.* Chicago: Childrens Press, 1974.

Porter, David, ed. *Biographical Dictionary of American Sports: Baseball.* Westport, CT: Greenwood, 1987.

Rudeen, Kenneth. *Roberto Clemente.* New York: Thomas Y. Crowell, 1974.

Wagenheim, Kal. *Clemente!* New York: Praeger Publishers, 1973.

INDEX

Picture Credits
AP/Wide World Photos: pp. 11, 22, 27, 41, 52, 56; National Baseball Library, Cooperstown, NY: pp. 17, 20, 32, 60; Pittsburgh Pirates: pp. 28, 47, 58; Copyright The Topps Company, Inc.: p. 24; UPI/Bettmann Newsphotos: 2, 8, 14, 30, 35, 36, 38, 42, 44, 48, 50, 55; U.S. Postal Service: p. 54

PETER C. BJARKMAN is the editor of the two-volume *Encyclopedia of Major League Baseball Team Histories,* and the author of *The Immortal Diamond: Baseball in American Literature and Culture,* as well as four other baseball history books. He is the chairman of the Latin America baseball committee for the Society for American Baseball Research., and is currently working on a history of Winter League baseball. Mr. Bjarkman has taught at Purdue University and the University of Colorado. He lives in West Lafayette, Indiana, with his wife, Dr. Ronnie Wilbur, a college professor.

JIM MURRAY, veteran sports columnist of the *Los Angeles Times,* is one of America's most acclaimed writers. He has been named "America's Best Sportswriter" by the National Association of Sportscasters and Sportswriters 14 times, was awarded the Red Smith Award, and was twice winner of the National Headliner Award. In addition, he was awarded the J. G. Taylor Spink Award in 1987 for "meritorious contributions to baseball writing." With this award came his 1988 induction into the National Baseball Hall of Fame in Cooperstown, New York. In 1990, Jim Murray was awarded the Pulitzer Prize for Commentary.

EARL WEAVER is the winningest manager in Baltimore Orioles history by a wide margin. He compiled 1,480 victories in his 17 years at the helm. After managing eight different minor league teams, he was given the chance to lead the Orioles in 1968. Under his leadership the Orioles finished lower than second place in the American League East only four times in 17 years. One of only 12 managers in big league history to have managed in four or more World Series, Earl was named Manager of the Year in 1979. The popular Weaver had his number 5 retired in 1982, joining Brooks Robinson, Frank Robinson, and Jim Palmer, whose numbers were retired previously. Earl Weaver continues his association with the professional baseball scene by writing, broadcasting, and coaching.